Build your career with NLP

DISCLAIMER

This information is provided and sold with the knowledge that the publisher and author do not offer any legal or other professional advice. In the case of a need for any such expertise consult with the appropriate professional. This book does not contain all information available on the subject. This book has not been created to be specific to any individual's or organizations' situation or needs. Every effort has been made to make this book as accurate as possible. However, there may be typographical and or content errors. Therefore, this book should serve only as a general guide and not as the ultimate source of subject information. This book contains information that might be dated and is intended only to educate and entertain. The author and publisher shall have no liability or responsibility to any person or entity regarding any loss or damage incurred, or alleged to have incurred, directly or indirectly, by the information contained in this book.

Thank you for downloading this book. Please review on Amazon for us so that I can make future versions even better. A portion of the proceeds from this book goes to American Cancer Society®. Thank you for you support. God bless.

Just for Downloading this book and showing your support, I wanna give you 2 of our other books, absolutely **FREE**. Just go to the link and subscribe and get **2 Free Books** for your support. Don't forget to give us **5 star Rating** so we can make better versions to help more people. Thank you guys for your support.

Click Here to Download-Free Website Traffic & How To Invest in The Stock Market

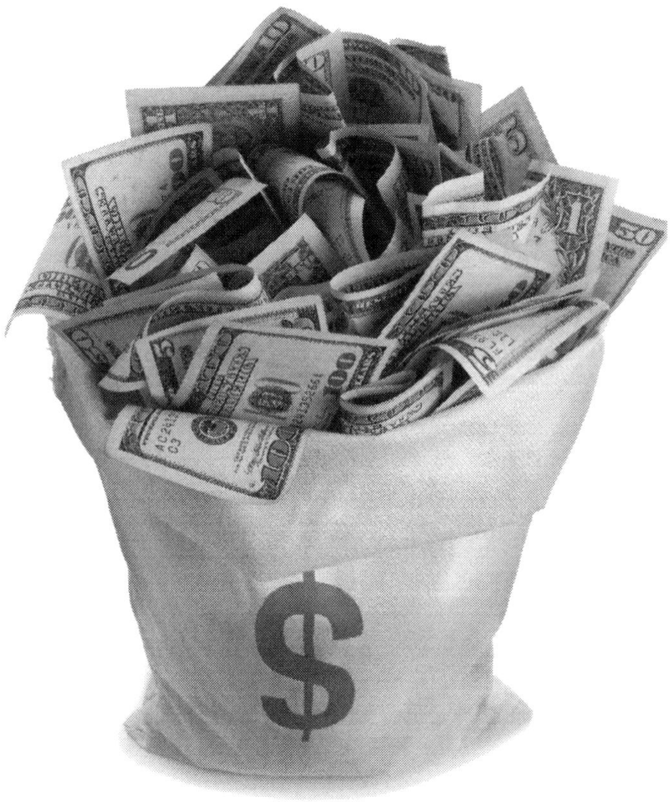

Table of Contents

Foreword 7

1. All About NLP 9
2. How Does NLP Help You Grow 13
3. How NLP Helps With Career 17
4. How NLP Helps With Relationships 21
5. How NLP Helps With Confidence 25
6. How NLP Helps With Habits 29
7. How NLP Helps With Fears 31
8. How NLP Helps With Languages 35
9. How NLP Helps With Productivity 39
10. The Trouble With Not Adjusting Your Mind 43

Wrapping Up 45

Foreword

The NLP systems provides for the circumstances to develop the individual excellence levels while also establishing the empowering belief of a particular system.

Chapter 1:
All About NLP

Synopsis

NLP is the short form version used when referring to Neuro Linguistic Programming. Simply put the NLP is the term used to describe the three basic systems within a vast array of connecting systems. These three basic systems are the neurology system, the language system, and the programming system.

The Basics

Basically the neurological system with the body is the one that regulates the different body functions while the language system of an individual determines how the said individual communicates and interacts with others around.

The third system which is the programming system determines the kind of world the individual creates for himself or herself based on the before mentioned systems.

Put together the three distinct systems complement each other to work towards the oneness of mind, language and behavior or interaction. All three systems interplay with each other to produce the images of the individual's own little "world."

Being a form of pragmatism the NLP is multi dimensional in its processing form and allows for the development of behavioral adjustments and competence with a touch of flexibility.

These inter twined systems also creates the possibility for the forming of strategic thinking and the understanding of the mental and cognitive which constitutes certain behavioral patterns in an individual.

The NLP systems also provides for the circumstances to develop the individual excellence levels while also establishing the empowering belief of a particular system. It also functions as a discovery tool to facilitate self discovery, exploring the individual's identity and also to create a self mission mindset.

There is also the element of spirituality involved as the NLP also provides the frame work for the individual to freely and with a higher level of understanding explore this part of the human existence. In essence NLP is not only about competence and excellence but it is also about discovering the potentials of wisdom and vision too.

Chapter 2:
How Does NLP Help You Grow

Synopsis

Everyone likes to be able to grow both mentally and physically. There are many ways of addressing this issue of growth; some are pretty easy and straight forward while others can be quite unnervingly complicated like NLP. Seemingly simple it has a lot of underlying complications and implications.

Behind It

Being able to truly discern the various levels of the understanding and thought process of one's self and of those around will create the possibility of being able to better relate to each other and transfer information more efficiently.

Everyone has different ways and forms of processing the information around them. This information is processed by the senses while include sight, smell, touch, hearing and taste.

When it comes to communication the sensors most used are the sense of sight which is then communicated through other skills or forms. These forms may include visual, audio, kina esthetic or a combination of these.

Being able to identify correctly the form used by the individuals on the receiving end of the information will ensure that the said information is correctly understood for what it is.

It would be a little more difficult to communicate when the NLP systems used by others are not quite the same as one's self. However this does not mean communication is impossible; it just means it may cause a few confusions before the matter is understood completely and easily. Therefore identifying which form is best suited to the individual would allow for the better and quicker absorption of information. If the form that is best suited is visual then perhaps being exposed to a lot of visually presented information would facilitate faster absorption.

If the mode of information is auditory then those that are better able to absorb auditory instructions or information would benefit. Similarly with kina esthetics which would require the involvement of touch and feel in order to be an effective tool of communication.

Chapter 3:
How NLP Helps With Career

Synopsis

Understanding the NLP of those around and playing to this advantage will always bring about great benefits. The better and more effectively information is used and given out, the more benefits can be derived.

Your Work

In the work place, understanding this is very important. If the communication methods currently used are not bringing forth the desired results, the other options should be looked into.

For instance, when communication with superiors, it would be prudent to take a little time to find out how they individually like receiving information.

These can vary from person to person, so a little research will go a long way. If visual effects are effective then ensure as much of the information disseminated is in the form of visual effects. For those who are more receptive to audio based information, then presenting information this way would garner better results. All this research should be done in a way that would play off the receptivity of the receiver.

When it comes to interacting with co workers and passing information around the same principal applies. If the mode of information used is receptive then the level of work achieved will be of better quality and quantity.

The work environment would then be better as all involved would understand and receive the information better and according to their receptiveness. When time is taken to understand the different information absorption capabilities of those around, the individual can then make the necessary adjustments to ensure this method is used.

Those interested to adopting the NLP method to advance their careers may consider taking up a short course of this nature. The courses offered normally encourage the participants to explore and develop the individual's own NLP techniques and models. A lot of practical scenarios are used to help the individual exercise the new found style of dispersing information.

Chapter 4:
How NLP Helps With Relationships

Synopsis

The uses of NLP in creating the ideal elements for successful relationships are very beneficial indeed. Studies have shown that people in general use different basis of NLP to think and experience their surroundings and perceptions. Learning how to successfully manipulate the information with reference to NLP can effectively causes changes in thoughts, behaviors, and beliefs.

Relationships

The mind processes the information and then dictates how the individual will react to something. The linguistic skills will provide the verbalization of the concept to others and also to express thoughts, then the programming will dictate the sequences of actions and the consequential outcome of the action taken.

Thus by adopting the NLP frame work into a relationship the outlook and approach to many aspects can help to prevent any negative elements from being manifested.

People become better equipped to handle disagreements and understand better the reasons behind a certain reaction or act. Choices are consciously made to approach disagreements in a different way so as to ensure the degree of negativity is decreased considerably.

This is because after many sessions of using this NLP method of addressing issues, the individual can then on an unconscious level pattern the behavior to be more positive in nature. Besides this the positive response will also become more relatively easy to exercise.

Many people who have tried the NLP method of dissecting and dispersing information have found that their stress levels have increasingly become less. People have also attested to being able to use the NLP to come up with newer and more innovative ways of working on their respective relationships in order to be able to have a more comfortable relationship. Because communication is often the area of contention is any relationship exploring the possibility of using NLP to learn how to better manage this aspect of a relationship is encouraged.

Chapter 5:
How NLP Helps With Confidence

Synopsis

Using the NLP method to address other aspects of an individual's life is found to be beneficial, therefore using it as a toll to address the confidence of an individual should be no different.

Self Assurance

Having a high level of confidence is certainly an advantage everyone can do with. The confidence gained using the NLP method can be just as powerful as confidence gained any other way. Once mastered, there are no limits to what can be achieved through the new level of confidence gained.

Many scientists have concluded that the confidence of an individual is often just a simple psychological toll that has either not been develop well or has been subjected to some level of battering. Thankfully this lack can be addressed and turned around using quite a few methods and one of which is NLP.

Perhaps the first and most important step is to acknowledge is that confidence is nothing to be daunted about. Confidence is just a tool that the limbic system is able to put forth for the use of the individual which ever say seen fit.

Therefore encouraging the visualization, audio form or any other sensor system that is predominant in processing information for the individual is what helps the individual to gain the confidence needed.

If visualization is the form most receptive to the individual then using this process the mind's eye can the project a confident persona that is accepted and termed popular. This can then transcend into reality because the mind has already registered the visualization as being a confident persona.

If the NLP of the individual is more of the audio relaying form then this media form should be constantly used to reinforce the confidence. Being exposed to as many positive and confidence audio presentations will allow the mind to absorb and practice what it has constantly been exposed to.

Chapter 6:

How NLP Helps With Habits

Synopsis

Some habits are good and some are bad. The bad habits are almost always hard to break or stop completely. However all is not lost as new research has found that the mind can be trained to reject or reprogram the bad habit actions until they don't exists anymore. This new discovery is called NLP.

Putting It To Work

Changing the perception of a pleasure derived from a bad habit to an unpleasant experience is one way of using the mind in the NLP way. Simply put it would seem that the mind is being tricked into a new line of thought which is intended to change the perception of something into another and by doing this it is hoped that the body will eventually associate the habit will unpleasantness and thus make it easier to reject.

When this initial stage is reached the next stage should be to create in the mind's eye the same perception toward the habit but in an even more intensified association. The idea here is to completely rid one's self of even the slightest urge to go back to the bad habit.

Train the mind to focus on other things the moment something connected to the habit surfaces. When the mind is able to do this the habit can be considered broken.

In the same way one can apply NLP to starting new and good habits. All it takes is to train the mind to identify, disseminate, and apply. This same pattern can be applied quite successfully. The key is to use a media form that is most able to convey the intended message to the brain successfully and effectively. Following these recommendations will in effect program the neuro patterns which in turn will direct the linguistic and communication elements.

Chapter 7:

How NLP Helps With Fears

Synopsis

Fear has no particular outward physical warning sign; it is more of a mental alert system which tells the body it is about to experience something negative and perhaps even painful. Though it seems simple enough to explain the impact of fear is just in the mind, most people are unable to come to terms with this perception.

Concerns

Using the NLP method which is the disassociation technique that reliever fears and removes unwanted emotional feelings, the individual is able to train the mind to replace these associations with other more positive elements. The mind is taught to substitute the fear factor with other more pleasant interpretations.

Some of the recommended ways to start this process would be to begin with finding a place free of distractions and concentrate on what normally bring on the fear factor.

Then this condition is recognized in the mind then the process of training the mind to disassociate itself from the fear and replace it with something else can then start.

Finding the element that starts the fear build up and then addressing it with more powerful feelings of confidence and safety may eventually help the mind to address the fear without actually submitting to it.

Some people may even want to try visualizing the fear and then "talking" it down until they are comfortably able to the fear without actually feeling the effects of it in the previously weaker position.

Some people consider this technique to be similar to playing mind games, but if it is found to be effective in combating the fear then these mind games are worth trying.

When a certain level of confidence is reached and one is comfortable with the fact that the said fear is no longer a dominant factor the actually experimenting facing the element that caused the fear will help to convince the individual that the fear previously experienced was unfounded.

Chapter 8:

How NLP Helps With Languages

Synopsis

Those who have mastered the NLP method of using language to the best advantage all attest to its fundamentally positive attributes. These can be divided into four main categories, which are sensory based fundamentals, Meta modules, Milton modules and the sleight of mouth patterns. There are already people out in the world who are already sensitive to the attributes of reading these various NLP languages.

More In Depth

Most people habitually speak the way they think which is probably derived from the various life experiences. Here is where these previously used patterns can be manipulated and changed at its core level to either enhance the style of decrease it, whichever is preferable. The direction the mind takes in a certain situation will dictate the speech patterns that are used. This then can be trained to a certain extent and even altered altogether through constant and conscious practice.

Conditioning the mind to respond to the language patterns in a certain way is the ideal scenario of the NLP system. One example popularly used to illustrate this, is the tone of voice used when making various kinds of statements. Changing the tone but maintaining the words will reflect different projections. The actual phrasing and structure also play an important role in influencing the desired outcome.

Directing the mind is another essential principle to acknowledge. In doing this many different facets can be used and experimented upon. However testing this theory may not always yield the desired results especially if the mind has not reached the conditioned level it should. Practicing delivery through the NLP method can teach an individual how to deliver a statement which will have lasting effects on the listener. This is a vital tool to have if the person is in the teaching or imparting information business.

Chapter 9:
How NLP Helps With Productivity

Synopsis

A lot of things are lost along the way because of the lack of proper communication or the total breakdown in communication. When this happens to effect the productivity of an individual or a team then the seriousness of this communication breakdown needs to be addressed. One way of doing so is by using the NLP method which many attest to being effective.

Getting More Done

Failing to "sell" an idea or concept effective and successfully can be detrimental to the vision of launching the said idea or concept. When there is no connection made between the various parties involved it would signify that the eventual productivity level would also be severely affected.

This will also lead to other undesirable effects like more unnecessary problems causing further delays from the low productivity levels.

Thus it would be prudent to realize that something must be done to enhance the communication between parties so that the productivity levels can then be at its optimum.

Identifying the behavior that is causing the productivity to stagnate is essential to deciding the method to address it. Besides identifying the behavioral patterns the signals that lead up to the pattern should also be noted.

Encouraging the individual to make the change to bring about a positive behavioral mind set which will now turn the focus towards better productivity levels. In some cases there may be a need to create other communication patterns for the purpose of increasing productivity if the initial changes are not up to par.

In some NLP sessions in the method, of addressing the negative issues the participant are told to identify the problematic area and mentally start the changing process.

Bringing the issues to the surface is also acknowledging the fact that the particular issue is the problem and not the overall person. When the necessary changes are embarked upon the byproduct of this change should be better productivity levels.

Chapter 10:
The Trouble With Not Adjusting Your Mind

Synopsis

Taking the time to learn new things that can create better things, feelings, connections, and other positive things in an individual's life is always worth pursuing. Thus with the same concept in mind not taking the opportunity to pursue the NLP method of making a positive change would indeed be a loss.

What You Ought To Know

When the conscious effort is not made to better the way information is accepted and distributed by the mind a lot of elements can be lost such as the extreme confidence that can be applied to all aspects of the individual's life, the hidden charisma that can be unleashed and perhaps also the fear factor that causes people to react the way they do. All possibility of improving all these areas in life could be lost because of the reluctance to try the NLP methods.

This self help teachings and techniques can be applied by anyone into the daily life thoughts to enhance any positive attributes and also discard the negativity in the person.

With the aid of the NLP method adjusting the mind will become a much easier and more natural process for the individual using this method. Extreme self confidence can be gained, amazing levels of public speaking skill can be developed, and deep negative issues can be addressed, all this done with a high percentage of success.

Wrapping Up

Being able to "train" the brain is a very effective way of addressing any problems and once this method is properly mastered there is almost nothing that cannot be addressed this way.

The most paralyzing element that most people overcome with NLP is the fear factor. The changes most people experience in being able to control the mind accordingly have been documented as phenomenal to say the least. Basically in controlling the mind, the rest will be easier.

Printed in Great Britain
by Amazon.co.uk, Ltd.,
Marston Gate.